World Issues

EQUAL OPPORTUNITIES

Fiona Macdonald

Belitha Press

WORLD ISSUES

DRUGS
EQUAL OPPORTUNITIES
GENETIC ENGINEERING
POVERTY
REFUGEES

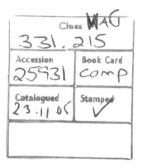

Produced by Roger Coote Publishing
Gissing's Farm, Fressingfield, Suffolk IP21 5SH, UK

First published in the UK in 2002 by Belitha Press
64 Brewery Road, London N7 9NT

A member of **Chrysalis** Books plc

Commissioning Editor: Jason Hook
Designer: Tim Mayer
Consultant: Jim Mulligan, CSV
Picture Researcher: Lynda Lines

ISBN: 1 84138 419 4

British Library Cataloguing in Publication Data for this book is available from
the British Library.

Printed in Hong Kong/China
10 9 8 7 6 5 4 3 2 1

Picture Acknowledgements
We wish to thank the following individuals and organizations for their help and assistance, and for
supplying material in their collections: Associated Press 7, 14 (Tony Talbot), 21 (Becker und Bredel),
31 (Max Nash), 35 (Peter Morrison), 38 (Maxim Marmur), 41 (Ben Margot); Corbis 9, 10 (Flip
Schulke), 34 (David and Peter Turnley), 44 (Bettmann); Corbis Stock Market 5 middle (Chuck
Savage), 40 (Lightscapes); Hutchison Library 3, 5 top (Robert Abermann), 5 bottom (Philip
Wolmoth), 12 (Nancy Durrell McKenna), 16 (Jeremy Horner), 18 (Eric Lawrie), 26 (Aymon Frank), 42
(Jeremy Horner); John Birdsall Photography front cover, 6; Popperfoto 1 (Reuters), 8, 13, 15
(Reuters), 17 (Reuters), 19 (Reuters), 23 (Reuters), 27 (PN2), 28 (Reuters), 29, 30 (Reuters), 33
(Reuters), 37, 45 (Reuters), 47 (Reuters); Press Association 4 (The Herald, Glasgow); Rex Features 25
(Richard Young), 32, 39 (Tony Kyriaco); Still Pictures 46 (Jorgen Schytte); Topham Picturepoint 11,
20, 22, 24, 36 (Press Association), 43 (Image Works). Artwork by Michael Posen. The pictures used in
this book do not show the actual people named in the case studies in the text, except on pages 4-5.

CONTENTS

Neil's Story

Neil Walkingshaw is a car mechanic. He is 35 years old and lives in Scotland with his wife and young son, Sean. In November 2001, he won a landmark case at an industrial tribunal – a special court that investigates serious disputes between employers and their employees.

NEIL HAD WORKED full-time for the same employer for over eight years before his son was born. His wife, Tracy, also had a job. Like other women workers in the UK, she was entitled to maternity leave – in her case, for six months. And, like many women, Tracy wanted to go back to work after her maternity leave was over.

Neil and Tracy planned to share the responsibility for looking after baby Sean, so Neil asked his employers whether he could work part-time. He said, 'I expected the company to at least discuss the matter and look at all the options, because women who had children had been offered their jobs part-time or other part-time jobs with the company, but I was told they couldn't get anyone to do it part-time along with me.

I offered to try and find someone for a job share, and I was told the paperwork would be too complicated and too messy.'

Neil felt he was left with no choice. He had to resign. Neil contacted the Equal Opportunities Commission, a body set up by the UK government in 1975 to enforce laws banning sex discrimination. They helped him take his case to the industrial tribunal. The tribunal decided that Neil had been discriminated against and awarded him £36 000 in compensation. When giving their decision, members of the tribunal remarked that Neil's employers 'gave no meaningful consideration' to his request to work part-time. They added that if a woman had made the same request, the company would probably have agreed.

After hearing the tribunal's decision, Neil commented: 'I'm glad I did this because there will be other guys in the same position who want to look after their kids. I hope this will encourage them to make sure they can do that.' Today, Neil works part-time for a different car repair company – and enjoys his other part-time task of looking after Sean.

Source: The Herald, Glasgow, 21 November 2001

Three areas of discrimination

Gender is not the only area in which people suffer from discrimination and a lack of equal opportunities.

RACE
In South Africa, many black and Asian people work as labourers, with white people as their supervisors. This happens even though the policy of discrimination called apartheid ended in 1991.

DISABILITY
Many people with disabilities have achieved high academic qualifications but find that success in their studies does not lead to a rewarding career – or to any job at all. In the UK only 31 per cent of disabled people of working age are in paid employment.

AGE
Older people are often assumed to be less productive than young workers. In times of economic crisis, they are usually among the first to be made redundant. In Western industrial societies, it can be particularly difficult for men over the age of 50 to find a job.

What Are Equal Opportunities?

The idea of 'equal opportunities' is closely linked to other important beliefs about how life should be lived – such as justice and tolerance. Equal opportunities involves sensitive issues including gender, race, religion, disability and age. It affects all levels of society, from government law-makers to children at school.

Today, these children play happily together. But will they all have equal opportunities to achieve their ambitions when they grow up? Or will some of them be discriminated against because of their gender, ethnic origin or religious beliefs?

The Employment Service

'The Employment Service is committed to Equal Opportunities. This means that we treat all applicants fairly, irrespective of ethnic origin, gender, marital status, sexual orientation, age, religion or disability.'

Source: A newspaper advertisement by The Employment Service, a UK government agency, December 2001

EQUAL OPPORTUNITIES MEANS different things to different people in different parts of the world. But whoever – and wherever – they are, most men and women agree that equal opportunities means treating everyone equally at work and in education and giving them a fair chance to make the best of their lives regardless of gender, race, age, disability and religion.

In some places, ignoring peoples' sexual identity (whether they are gay or not) and their married or family status (whether they have a husband, wife or children) is also included in definitions of equal opportunities. People should also have the right to expect equal pay for equal work.

Do we have equal opportunities?

Most people think equal opportunities is a good idea. But equality is seldom achieved – at least, not completely. Law-makers and campaigners do not all agree on when or how equal opportunities should be introduced or enforced. Also, many individuals still benefit from unequal opportunities, in business or in institutions such as the law courts and the armed forces. Often, they are the people with the most power to create change. Until they are willing

DEBATE - Are equal opportunities policies really necessary?

- Yes, it is essential that everyone is given the same opportunities in work. Equal opportunities policies are the only way to achieve this.
- No, equal opportunities policies help minority groups, but not the majority. They mean employing the second-best people. They are not necessary – all we really need is common sense.

to question some of their work practices and perhaps give up some of their privileges, it seems unlikely that there will be equal opportunities for all.

But equal opportunities activists keep campaigning, and many countries have recently passed equal opportunities laws. In this book, we will investigate how equal opportunities policies are changing the way in which men and women work, in many parts of the world.

Protesters in 1976 at a rally in Springfield, Illinois, USA. They are campaigning for the Equal Rights Amendment (ERA), which would give equal rights to men and women by law (see page 11).

Why are laws necessary?

Today, many countries have laws giving equal rights to men and women workers and to particular groups of employees such as people with disabilities.
They also have laws banning racial discrimination in all areas of life, including work and education. Some countries have laws protecting religious minorities from harassment in the workplace and elsewhere.

Why were there no laws in the past?

Before the 1960s, there were few equal opportunities laws. Most policy-makers thought they were unnecessary. Some thought equal opportunities was a moral issue which individuals should decide for themselves. Others believed that laws would not work, since they could not change peoples' attitudes. A few refused to give up old prejudices, saying that equal opportunities policies would destroy 'traditional ways of life'.

Some politicians hoped that discrimination would gradually vanish from the workplace – and the whole of society – as men and women began to work for the same companies and people from different ethnic groups moved to the same neighbourhoods. They believed that as different people came to know each other, they would become 'colour-blind' or 'gender-blind', and automatically behave in a fair, equal way. Others thought that the free market would create equal opportunities: businesses would not care whether employees were male or female, black or white, old or young, with disabilities or without, so long as they worked well.

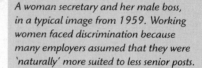

A woman secretary and her male boss, in a typical image from 1959. Working women faced discrimination because many employers assumed that they were 'naturally' more suited to less senior posts.

Ella Watson, a poor, black cleaner in American government offices in 1942, poses in front of the American flag.

What changed peoples' minds?

However, discrimination continued. Almost everywhere, top jobs were given to able-bodied men from the majority ethnic groups. Women and people from ethnic minorities were still working mainly in low-status, poorly paid jobs. People with disabilities or those who were over 50 found it hard to get work at all.

Campaigners came to realize that equal opportunities would never be achieved by hoping that disadvantaged people would just 'fit in'. Discrimination was not a private moral issue for individuals alone. It was a political problem which affected everyone. Equality at work could only be achieved by changing the balance of power within society – and that would require new laws.

How Did Equal Opportunities Begin?

During the 1950s and 1960s, several factors combined to make governments in the USA and Europe think more carefully about how different groups in society should be protected by law.

BY THE 1960s, Western industrial economies were growing fast. Companies needed good employees and were prepared to treat them well. There was also a new generation of well-educated young people who wanted rewarding careers. Young men were not prepared to settle for low-paid, low-status jobs, and young women did not all want to be mothers and home-makers.

The terrible experiences of the Second World War had led to support for peaceful international organizations, such as the United Nations (UN), and an interest in human rights of all kinds – including equal opportunities. In some European countries, such as Sweden and Denmark, progressive political attitudes and the development of the welfare state enabled women to work on almost equal terms with men – although less was done to help ethnic minorities.

American civil rights leader, Martin Luther King, speaking at a civil rights rally in the 1960s. His campaigns for an end to discrimination led to important new laws in many parts of the world.

Women campaigning in 1952 for equal pay. They wear masks to avoid being recognized by their employers.

Different cultures

Some nations have different cultural and religious beliefs and do not have equal opportunities policies. They believe their own laws will produce the best life for all their workers. The Taliban rulers of Afghanistan received worldwide criticism for their treatment of women – such as banning women nurses and teachers from work – until their removal from power in 2002.

What was the Civil Rights Act?

In the USA, black Americans, Native Americans and Hispanics faced unequal treatment at work and in their everyday lives. From 1955, black Americans staged protests against discrimination. In 1963, led by the inspirational preacher Martin Luther King, they joined with many thousands of white supporters in mass demonstrations demanding equal rights. These forced the government to pass the USA's most important equal opportunities law, the Civil Rights Act of 1964.

American women played a key part in civil rights protests and also made demands of their own. Since 1923, female politicians had been leading campaigns calling for the Equal Rights Amendment (ERA) to the American Constitution, which would give women legal equality with men. By the 1960s, they had been joined by radical feminists, who called for a complete change in traditional gender roles and family life, as well as equal

opportunities at work. In 1963, women won the right to equal pay for equal work. Further employment rights were guaranteed by the Civil Rights Act the following year.

In the years following the Civil Rights Act, laws were introduced in the USA banning job discrimination against people who had disabilities or were over 40 years old. Religious discrimination was also outlawed. Since 1991, Americans who feel they have suffered discrimination have been able to seek financial damages. Other countries, including Canada, Australia and many in the European Union (EU), have followed this example.

A Russian woman doctor. In Soviet times, women had equal educational opportunities with men, and were encouraged to have professional careers. By 1990, over 70 per cent of Russian doctors were women.

Role of religion

Religious ideologies can affect equal opportunities. The lowest numbers of women working for wages are in Algeria (8 per cent of the work-force) and in Afghanistan, Oman and Saudi Arabia (each 9 per cent). In all these countries, strict interpretations of Islam are held by the people in power.

Source: Joni Seager, The State of Women in the World Atlas

Did political change create equality?

During the twentieth century, there were revolutions in many parts of the world. New left-wing and communist governments claimed to be fighting for equality for all their citizens. Many people hoped that such political movements would bring equal opportunities more quickly than

new laws. But looking back, we can see that many changes made in the name of 'equality' or 'freedom' failed to bring equal opportunities for all.

For example, after the Russian Revolution in 1917, women in the Soviet Union were given equal political rights with men. They had the right to work outside the home and to receive a good education. State-run industries relied on women working side-by-side with men, and female workers were praised as 'real Soviet women, proud to be good mothers and good workers'. But at the same time, Soviet laws restricted individual freedoms such as the right to protest against the government and the right to set up your own business.

After the Second World War, many Soviet women trained for skilled professional careers. Their lives were interesting and materially comfortable, but they were never paid as much as men. Like Soviet women working on farms and in factories, they were also expected to run a home and care for children as well as work full-time.

What happened in China?

The 1948 Communist Revolution in China also promised equality for its citizens. But political change failed to alter traditional attitudes to women. As one observer commented: 'Chinese parents want boys rather than girls, so from the moment they are born, females are made to feel unwanted. In later life, they may be married off to an older, abusive husband, or even sold.'

In the late twentieth century, both China and Russia (after the break-up of the Soviet Union) introduced capitalist economic policies. These encouraged 'freedom' and 'enterprise'. But they also had a damaging effect on women and other disadvantaged groups. For example, in 1995, women's wages in Russia were 40 per cent of men's. In Soviet times they had averaged 70 per cent.

Since 1995, large numbers of Chinese men have left the countryside to find better-paid jobs in cities, leaving women to do over 70 per cent of the work on farms. The government's new economic rules mean that farm prices have fallen dramatically, and women simply cannot survive. China is home to 21 per cent of the world's women, but accounts for over 50 per cent of the world's female suicides.

A group of Red Guards (young communist activists) in Beijing, 1967. Although communist theory taught that women were equal with men, traditional Chinese attitudes towards women have proved stronger.

Are Working Women Equal With Men?

Despite the introduction of equal opportunities laws, there is no country where the majority of women workers are treated completely equally with men. Although there are many successful working women, and some outstanding high achievers, women workers almost always receive lower pay.

IN THE USA, for example, white women earn an average 65 per cent, black women earn 58 per cent and Hispanic women earn 52 per cent of white men's earnings. Around the world, the work performed by women is usually less skilled and therefore less secure than the work performed by men. Women are less likely than men to belong to trade unions, which could bargain for pay rises and protect their rights. They are much more likely than men to be employed on temporary and part-time contracts.

Women in Vermont, USA, take part in a demonstration on Equal Pay Day, 1999. Depite equal opportunities laws, average women's pay in the USA is still much lower than men's.

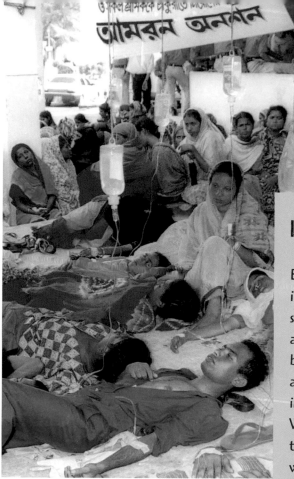

Women workers in an Export Processing Zone in Bangladesh take part in a hunger strike, supported by some of their male colleagues. They are demanding better pay and the right to belong to trade unions.

In economic crises, women and older people are the groups most likely to be unemployed. In some countries, women are treated as pools of 'disposable' labour – if their job contract ends, their husbands or their parents are expected to support them. In many countries, only men are expected to earn a steady 'family wage'.

How many women are wage-earners?

Since the 1970s, increasing numbers of women have worked for wages. By the late 1990s, women made up around 36 per cent of the wage-earning work-force worldwide. But many women still work at home, often unpaid. Some follow traditional occupations, such as farming or craftwork. Others help their parents or husbands, working in small family enterprises.

As economic globalization increases, and multinational corporations search for the cheapest, least powerful employees, large numbers of women are being employed in low-paid piecework in their homes. They often have to work in cramped or unhealthy conditions and are not entitled to any benefits.

What is women's work?

In every country, certain jobs are recognized as 'women's work', while others are believed to 'belong' to men. But these ideas generally vary from country to country. Whether a job is 'male' or 'female' depends on local customs and traditions. These can sometimes be extremely surprising. In India, for example, women work as road-builders – a typical man's job in many parts of the world.

The jobs most frequently done by women around the world have developed from women's unpaid tasks within the home, such as nursing, teaching and child-care. Caring for the sick and educating children are obviously responsible and important jobs, yet they have low status and poor prospects because they are done by

women. The same is true for all other occupations seen as 'women's work'. Where women work in jobs that are also done by men, they generally occupy the least senior positions. These positions also have low status – mostly because they are associated with women.

What is the maid trade?

Some women workers are treated with total disrespect by their employers and are at risk of sexual harassment and physical abuse. The 'maid trade' provides a good example. Over 1.5 million Asian women work as household servants – cooking and cleaning are typical female jobs – in the Middle East and in rich Asian regions such as Hong Kong. Most do not speak the local language and are ignorant of the law. They are isolated within their employers' homes and have little control

Women building a road in Rajasthan, India. Women have proved themselves capable of doing many different kinds of work, in spite of traditional, stereotyped opinions.

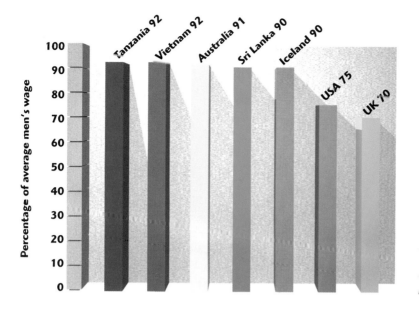

Tanzania 92   Vietnam 92   Australia 91   Sri Lanka 90   Iceland 90   USA 75   UK 70

Percentage of average men's wage

This graph shows the average women's wage as a percentage of the average men's wage in countries from different parts of the world.

over their lives. Many have alleged that their employers ill-treat them. Women are also tricked into applying for jobs as maids, then forced to work as prostitutes. Some poor families hand over girls to dealers, who promise to find them work without saying what it will be. Prostitution is organized by men and controlled by male violence.

Are women paid equally to men?

Because of their low status, jobs labelled as women's work are badly paid. Even where men and women do similar jobs, they often do not receive equal pay. Women in countries with equal opportunities laws have successfully challenged this several times. In one famous case, a group of school dinner ladies in the UK won the right to be treated as permanent employees, like dustmen employed by the same organization. This entitled them to benefits such as holiday pay.

But discrimination remains. In the UK, women earn on average only 70 per cent as much as men. Women from ethnic minority groups find themselves doubly disadvantaged, because they often work

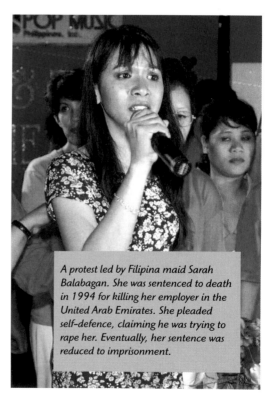

A protest led by Filipina maid Sarah Balabagan. She was sentenced to death in 1994 for killing her employer in the United Arab Emirates. She pleaded self-defence, claiming he was trying to rape her. Eventually, her sentence was reduced to imprisonment.

in the lowest-paid women's jobs at the lowest-paid grades. On average, black women workers in the UK earn 23 per cent less than white women and 37 per cent less than black men.

Women workers in Peru. They are spinning wool, using traditional wooden spindles. Many women's jobs today are still based on traditional female tasks, such as child-care, and on traditional female craft skills.

Why don't both sexes do the same work?

In most countries, women have a smaller choice of jobs than men. Women have traditionally worked in a limited number of occupations, and this pattern continues even in countries where there are equal opportunities laws.

In the past, it was assumed by women's families and employers that certain occupations were not suitable for them. Reasons for this view included the idea that women were physically or mentally weaker, sometimes backed up by religious arguments or medical taboos.

In a few countries – including Bolivia, Lesotho, Syria and Zaire – husbands still have the right to ban their wives' choice of work or to forbid them from going out to work at all. But today in most countries, these sorts of attitudes are less important than three other factors. These are lack of education, lack of capital and the burden of women's domestic responsibilities.

Why is education important?

Over 600 million women – twice as many as men – have never learnt to read or write. In poor countries, fewer girls than boys go to school, and they stay in education for a shorter time. This is either because they are believed to be 'not worth' educating – when they marry, they will leave the family home – or because they are needed to help around the home or care for younger siblings. In South Asia, for example, 47 per cent of girls leave school before they are 10 years old, compared with 39 per cent of boys. In the Sahel region of Africa, fewer than 15 per cent of university students are women.

Is poverty a factor?

In some countries, poverty, inheritance laws and traditional customs restrict women's access to land or other forms of wealth. This limits their chances of going into business on their own. Even in countries with equal opportunities

laws, women complain that it is much harder for them to borrow money to start a company than it would be for a man.

Where poverty is combined with domestic responsibilities, a career can be impossible. Many women in poor rural communities spend their time caring for children, growing food and performing chores such as gathering firewood or collecting water. They work all day long, but not for pay. In comparison, working women's lives in industrialized regions such as the EU are very comfortable. But both groups of women find their opportunities limited by the need to care for homes and families.

Young girls carry heavy brass pots full of water to their family homes, in India in 2000. In spite of modern technology, millions of women and girls have to spend their days performing hard, boring tasks. They have no chance of an education or a career.

Limited choice

In a 1990 survey of six EU states, over half of all working women were employed in just six areas of the economy (retailing; healthcare; public administration; teaching; social and cultural; banking and finance). Men in the same countries worked in 58 different areas.

This single mother is fortunate. She is able to use a computer to work from home and care for her young children at the same time. But many women still find it difficult to combine family life with a career.

Are career women successful?

There are increasing numbers of successful career women, but they are still in a minority compared with successful men. In the UK, for example, only 15 per cent of top civil servants, and only 5 per cent of judges, are women.

Lack of education means that most women worldwide have no chance of competing with men. But even in countries such as the USA, Portugal and the UK – where there are now more female university students than male – many clever, ambitious women still do not succeed in careers. Most women find it very difficult to combine a career with having children and leading a 'normal' family life. Long hours, night shifts and the difficulty of finding reliable child-care create serious problems for working mothers – especially if they are lone parents.

What is the glass ceiling?

Successful career women also complain of peoples' attitudes towards them. Many say that they feel excluded from the traditional male work culture – not just in physically-demanding jobs such as heavy industry, but also among groups of senior male executives.

Women use terms like 'sticky floor' and 'glass ceiling' to describe the invisible barriers of suspicion and prejudice that they feel are placed in the way of their progress by male managers.

Successful women also face criticism, and sometimes open hostility, from colleagues. Some women find that men feel threatened by the female 'invasion' of their male working environment and resent having to take orders from women with power. Some men in turn allege that women are not tough enough to compete in the male world of big business – or alternatively complain that successful women are unnaturally hard and unfeminine.

But equal opportunities are very complex. Not only men, but also childless women, employed by companies with equal opportunities policies, have recently complained that working mothers receive unfair advantages.

DEBATE – Do mothers deserve special treatment?

In 2001, police constable Michelle Chew, a mother, won a case against her employers after they insisted that she work early-morning, late-evening and night-time shifts. An employment tribunal decided that this amounted to sex discrimination against women, who typically had greater child-care responsibilities than men. Reactions were mixed. Which of the following two views do you agree with?

- PC Chew: 'This is not about letting parents pick and choose to do only the nice shifts, it's about making it possible for them to work at all.'
- A representative of employers' organization, the Institute of Directors: 'This will breed resentment among men and among childless women.'

Source: The Herald, Glasgow, 21 November 2001

German electronics engineer Tanja Kreil was refused employment working on a weapons system for the army – a traditionally male–dominated profession. In 2000, she took her case to the European Court of Justice, claiming sex discrimination, and won.

Is women's work changing?

At the start of the new millennium, no one can deny that women's working lives are very different from 50 years before. In industrialized countries, women have proved that they can succeed in a wide range of traditionally male occupations, from astronauts and airline pilots to surgeons and sports superstars. Women with business skills now set up their own companies and find work in new kinds of careers such as communications and the media.

But they are still a small minority compared with men. In the UK in 2001, for example, only 57 out of the 100 top companies had even one woman as a board member.

In developing countries, educated women can train as doctors and college lecturers. By the mid-1990s, around half of all university teachers in Cuba, Namibia, Thailand and several islands in the Caribbean were women. Women in South America, Africa and Asia have joined together in co-operative schemes to harvest and market farm produce and their own craftwork. In order to help finance these businesses, they have set up a special network of banks which offer small loans to women. Over 90 per cent of the Grameen Bank of Bangladesh's clients are women. The Self-Employed Women's Association Co-operative Bank of India lends to women only. Worldwide, women's banks help over half a million customers each year.

UK athlete Denise Lewis, gold medallist in the heptathlon at the 2000 Olympics in Sydney, Australia, is just one of many women who have proved that they can succeed at the highest level.

Gro Harlem Brundtland (left), now director of the World Health Organization, joins in a teaching song with family-planning workers in India.

Can women succeed in politics?

Women have become more involved in politics of all kinds – from radical protest groups to mainstream political parties. But most women in politics serve as ordinary members of parliaments or other assemblies, where they are usually in a minority. In 1997, for example, women held 62 out of 535 seats in the US Congress and 120 out of 651 seats in the UK parliament.

However, a few tough and ambitious women have risen to become heads of government. They include Golda Meir of Israel (1969–1974), Margaret Thatcher of the UK (1979–1990) and Benazir Bhutto of Pakistan (1993–1996). In 1986, Gro Harlem Brundtland of Norway led

Date for equality

The UN estimates that, at the current rate of progress, women worldwide will have to wait until the year 2490 to achieve equality with men in high-paid, high-power, high-prestige positions at work.

Source: Joni Seager, The State of Women in the World Atlas

the first government in the world where women ministers outnumbered men. Slowly, women politicians have helped to improve equal opportunities in many countries. As Texan politician Sissy Farenthold once declared: 'You change laws by changing law-makers.'

Why Is There Racial Discrimination?

According to biologists, there is only one race – the human race. Yet everywhere, men and women discriminate against others who they think are different from themselves – in ethnic origins, nationality, language, skin colour or membership of clan or tribe.

OFTEN, THERE IS discrimination by majority communities against minorities who live in the same area. The rulers of Iraq have discriminated against Kurdish minorities in their country for many years. In the past, especially in Australia, the Americas and many British Empire territories, colonists arrived in a new land, imposed their own laws and culture and took over the native peoples' lands. This led to a history of discrimination against native peoples.

Wherever it happens, ethnic or racial discrimination is founded on ignorance. Almost always, it is also closely linked to power. People who have jobs, land or wealth rarely want to give them up, and they sometimes fear that anyone who is 'different' will take these things from them. In Germany, for example, workers of Turkish origin do not have rights to full citizenship, even though they were born and educated in Germany, work there and pay taxes.

A Kurdish woman and her baby wait at the Turkish border for transport to a refugee camp in 1991, after being expelled from their home in Iraq.

Diane Abbott and Paul Boateng are high-profile members of the small group of UK MPs from ethnic minority communities.

A white man's club

The European Union has been called 'a white man's club':

- It has no laws protecting people from racial discrimination at work to match its laws on sex discrimination.
- Some member states classify people of non-white origin as 'migrants' or 'immigrants', even if they were born in these states.
- It requires people from Africa, Asia, the Middle East and the Caribbean to have visas to enter.

In 1996, EU leaders issued a declaration condemning racism and xenophobia (fear of foreigners), but this has not led to strong new laws.

What role do people in power play?

People in power sometimes persuade themselves that those from different backgrounds are incapable of high achievement, because they are uneducated, less 'civilized' or lacking in experience. In 2001, the UK had only 12 Members of Parliament (MPs) from ethnic minorities. If MPs were elected to reflect the proportions of different groups among voters, there should have been 40.

People from minority communities face discrimination in housing, schooling, healthcare and work. Their struggle for equal opportunities has been backed by

politicians and community leaders, who argue that each person should be respected as an individual human being. Religious leaders have taught that a person's worth has nothing to do with their outward appearance or national origin, but lies in qualities such as kindness or devotion to duty. In Europe, the USA and many other countries, civil rights laws prohibit discrimination. Yet, equal opportunities for people of different backgrounds or racial groups have still not been truly achieved anywhere in the world.

Mineworkers in South Africa. During apartheid, many black workers accepted dangerous conditions deep underground in order to earn wages to support their families back in the homelands.

Apartheid

From 1948 to 1991, the white South African government had a policy of apartheid, or racial separation. Black people were denied basic civil rights, and millions were forced from their homes and jobs and resettled in 'homelands' – barren regions with no roads, power or water supplies, few schools and hospitals, no fields or farms, no industries, and no opportunities for paid work.

What happened in the past?

From the sixteenth century, European colonists settled in countries all over the world. Some Europeans sincerely believed they could bring 'civilization' to local peoples. Others used this idea to disguise their real motives – seeking wealth and political power. As a result, local peoples suffered. Their economies were disrupted and their traditional skills devalued. They lost control of their land and were denied education and healthcare.

When Europeans first settled in South America, religious scholars discussed whether the indigenous people were truly human and whether they had souls. These were not just religious concerns. By treating local people as inferiors, European settlers were able to claim that they were 'helping' them by taking over their lands. This view of non-Europeans as sub-human was also used to justify the thriving trade in black slaves from Africa to the USA and the Caribbean. This was one of the most terrible examples of unequal opportunities at work.

How does the past affect the present?

Slavery was abolished in the USA in 1865. But although racist attitudes were increasingly condemned, they did not go away. Millions of black American citizens were left poor, uneducated

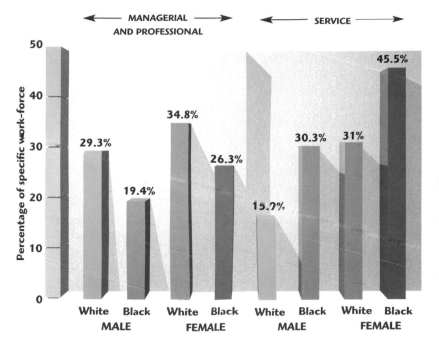

Percentage of specific work–force

50

45.5%

40

34.8%

30.3% 31%
29.3%   30
26.3%

19.4%   19.7%
20

10

0

White Black   White Black   White Black   White Black
MALE   FEMALE   MALE   FEMALE

This graph shows the percentage of the total white male, black male, white female and black female work–forces over the age of 16 working in two job areas in the USA.

Source: US Bureau of Labor

and in low-level jobs. By the middle of the twentieth century, European countries were losing their empires, but they maintained close links with the countries they had once ruled. When there was a labour shortage in the UK after the Second World War, workers were recruited from the Indian sub-continent and the Caribbean.
These workers, however, were not welcomed as equals when they arrived. Today, some of these workers, and their descendants, are still disadvantaged in housing, education, healthcare – and equal opportunities at work.

Many of those who arrived in the UK from the Caribbean after 1945 found work on the buses and railways. Today, their descendants are still working in public transport, mostly in low-paid, low-status jobs. There are about 20 million white males in the UK and around half a million Afro-Caribbean males. Yet, 18 per cent of men of Afro-Caribbean descent work in transport, and only 9 per cent of white men.

Some of the 492 men who sailed in 1948 from the Caribbean on the first 'migrant ship' carrying people to live and work in the UK. They are shown looking at job advertisements in a newspaper.

A Taiwanese waiter serves tapioca ('bubble') tea at a restaurant in New York's Chinatown. Many big cities have areas where people from one ethnic group live and work closely together.

What is a multicultural society?

Many societies now claim to be multicultural, and this is usually assumed to be a good thing. Being multicultural means respecting different peoples' beliefs and traditions, giving them each equal importance and making sure that none of them oppresses or destroys the others. The aim is to promote tolerance and understanding and to increase each member of the community's sense of security and self-confidence. However, equal opportunities campaigners have recently questioned whether multiculturalism really does help end racism and discrimination.

Does multiculturalism cause racism?

Some people argue that multiculturalism does not look deeply enough at the causes of racial discrimination. They also argue that multicultural policies keep different ethnic groups separate from one another.

At present, families with the same ethnic background often live close together. At an individual level, this may bring benefits. People find it convenient to be close to shops selling their preferred foods, clothes, newspapers or music and to have their own place of worship nearby. But for society as a whole, this can lead to worrying divisions, and sometimes to outbreaks of violence between rival groups who are intolerant of other people's way of life.

These divisions between separate communities are often continued into the workplace, leading to a lack of career opportunities for some people and to racial stereotyping.

Keeping people separate can also lead to abuses. For example, many Asian women work in Western countries as sewing-machinists and garment-makers. They often perform this work in their own homes or in cramped factories known as sweatshops (often owned by Asian businessmen). They are often exploited and underpaid, because they are isolated and do not belong to trade unions or other organizations which might be able to protect them. Some do not speak Western languages. Many have no knowledge of how to complain or how to assert their right to equal opportunities.

Victorious black American athletes give the Black Power salute at the 1968 Olympic Games. Their gesture shocked many people, but won valuable publicity for the campaign for equal opportunities.

Black is beautiful

In the 1960s and 1970s, some black Americans felt dissatisfied with the progress made by the civil rights movement – even after new equal opportunities laws had been passed. They set up the Black Power movement, for black people only, to campaign more militantly. They argued that black Americans should stop campaigning alongside liberal whites and should use all their energies to improve their own communities. They campaigned to win greater respect for black culture, using slogans such as 'black is beautiful'.

What is institutional racism?

In most countries today, the most powerful ethnic group controls all important state institutions – from schools and the Civil Service, to the army and police. Generally, these institutions do not deliberately discriminate against any group in society and do not intend to be racist. But they discriminate nevertheless.

Institutional racism has been described as 'policies and procedures within institutions that deny equal treatment to members of ethnic minority groups'. Valerie Amos, formerly Chief Executive of the Equal Opportunities Commission, explains: 'Historically, an environment has existed in which the favouring of individuals from certain groups (e.g. white men) has not been challenged because it is a norm. So, 'negative' discrimination, in favour of particular groups, became institutionalized.'

Equal opportunities campaigners have long claimed that 'institutional' racism exists. In the UK, they recently won support after investigations into one of the country's most important institutions, the police. In the 1990s, the Metropolitan Police Force was accused of institutional racism for failing to act after black student Stephen Lawrence was murdered in London in a random and unprovoked attack by a group of young, white, racist males. Government statistics show that Asians are 50 times more likely to suffer racist attacks than whites, and Afro-Caribbeans 36 times more likely.

Are there equal opportunities for jobs?

Many equal opportunities campaigners argue that simply offering people equal chances to apply for jobs still discriminates against disadvantaged groups in society. They say that disadvantaged people need to be

Three young white men are led past police barriers and groups of protesters to answer questions at the 1998 enquiry into the murder of black student Stephen Lawrence.

Captain Justin Butah, an officer in 1998 in the Household Cavalry, a prestigious part of the British Army. Since the 1990s, the British Army has made a positive effort to attract ethnic minority recruits.

given extra help to get a good education and learn useful skills. Otherwise they will remain at a disadvantage in their search for work.

To make sure that everyone really does have an equal chance of a rewarding career, campaigners for equal opportunities suggest 'positive' or 'affirmative' action. This might include free training and extra unpaid leave. It might also include major cultural, legal and financial reforms to remove prejudice and inequality from society as a whole. Campaigners argue that equal opportunities policies should be judged not by their good intentions, but by their practical results.

Reading and writing

In one industrial tribunal case, two Pakistani men living in the UK were asked to complete application forms for labouring jobs with a car manufacturing company in their own handwriting. This was the company's standard procedure for all people applying to work for them. But neither of the men could read and write in English, so they were unable to complete the forms and did not get the jobs. An industrial tribunal decided that the company was guilty of race discrimination, because being able to read and write in English was not a necessary qualification for basic labouring work.

Arthur Ashe (1943–1993) was the first black male tennis player to achieve a world ranking. He won the US Open Championship in 1968 and Wimbledon in 1975. He used his sporting success to work for equal opportunities for black people.

Can people from ethnic minorities succeed?

In Europe, the USA and many other parts of the world, men and women from minority ethnic groups are achieving great success. Their numbers are still small, but they are growing.

Racial discrimination in institutions and in society as a whole leaves a wide 'cultural divide'. Members of minority groups have to cross this if they want to achieve success. There is pressure to conform to certain expectations of speech and appearance. The American tennis star Arthur Ashe complained of the stress he suffered from being 'an ambassador' for the black community in the USA. Everywhere he went, he felt it was his duty to do nothing that might cause others to criticize black people. He also admitted to toning down his regional accent, so that it would be more 'acceptable' to listeners.

How does racism affect job opportunities?

This pressure to 'fit in' can also limit job opportunities. Skin colour is one of the most obvious differences between people and is instantly apparent – even though it tells us nothing about a person. Even so, many institutions and companies are wary of hiring people from minority groups, in case they do not 'fit in'. This is not logical, since the majority of non-white young people in Europe and the USA were born and educated there.

Job applicants from ethnic minorities can, of course, be better educated than applicants from the majority community. In the UK in the late 1990s, Asian school students achieved better exam results on average than white students. But even where job applicants from minority groups are well educated, they can still find it difficult to win acceptance. This can lead to unequal recruitment in many professions. For example, in the UK in the mid-1990s only 1.6 per cent of police officers came from ethnic minority groups. In contrast, 5 per cent of men of Indian ethnic origin were doctors, compared with only 0.7 per cent of white men. Ethnic minority doctors were, however, likely to be recruited for the least popular areas of medicine, such as mental health and the care of the elderly.

Singer Gloria Estefan with children in New York. They are looking at a website belonging to a community project designed to improve educational opportunities for members of the Hispanic ethnic group in the USA.

How Does Religion Affect Equal Opportunities?

A person's identity is made up of many strands – including ethnic or national background, gender, age and religious beliefs. It is hard to separate one strand completely from the others. Religion is often closely linked to politics and to issues of race or national origin. For this reason, it is rare to find discrimination against individuals or communities based simply on religion alone.

HOWEVER, PEOPLE WHO hold religious views which do not fit in with the majority views of the country where they work may face discrimination. The Soviet Union, for example, was officially an atheist state.

Jewish people who expressed a wish to emigrate from the Soviet Union to Israel – which had been founded in 1948 as a homeland for all Jews – were treated as political dissidents. Their promotion at work was blocked, and some lost their jobs.

During the 1980s, Soviet leader Mikhail Gorbachev introduced new freedoms to the Soviet Union. For the first time for almost a century, members of all religious groups, like these Jewish elders, had equal opportunities to practise their faith.

Members of the Royal Ulster Constabulary on parade in 2000. In the past, recruits came mostly from the Protestant religious majority in Northern Ireland

The Soviet authorities argued that by expressing a wish to emigrate they were behaving like traitors.

How can religion and politics be linked?

Belonging to a minority religious group can restrict work opportunities in other ways. In Northern Ireland, in the early twentieth century, many of the largest companies were controlled by members of the Protestant faith, who were the majority in the country. Most Protestant companies refused to employ Roman Catholics. This was not solely because of their religion, but because they assumed they would have political sympathies with Irish Republicans – a group who wanted Northern Ireland to break away from the UK and become part of the Republic of Ireland, a separate, independent state.

Today, Northern Ireland is the only part of the UK where there are laws against religious discrimination. The Fair Employment Protection Act of 1976 requires all employers with more than ten staff to monitor the religious balance of their work-force and regularly review their employment practices for any signs of discrimination.

When religion is linked to war and terrorism, this can also cause a backlash against workers of a particular faith.

Remembering rights

In the USA, the Civil Rights Act of 1964 prohibits workplace discrimination based on religion, as well as on national origin, race, colour or sex. After the terrorist attacks on 11 September 2001, the American Equal Employment Opportunity Commission (EEOC) issued a reminder to employers which included the following:

'The law's prohibitions include harassment or any other employment action based on any of the following:

● Harassing an individual because he or she is Arab or practises Islam
● Harassing a woman wearing *hijab* (a body covering and headscarf worn by some Muslims)
● Refusing to promote an employee because he or she attends a mosque.'

Source: US EEOC Website, 15 October 2001

After attacks by Muslim terrorists on the USA on 11 September 2001, some American Muslims faced hostility or harassment from work colleagues. Because they were Muslims, like the terrorists, they were accused of being anti-American.

Inspector Raj Kohli, a Sikh, discusses the progress of a police operation with colleagues. By the late twentieth century, officers from several ethnic and religious minority groups had risen to senior ranks in the UK's police forces, although their numbers remained small.

DEBATE - Is this fair?

In the UK, Section 11 of the Employment Act 1989 allows Sikhs wearing turbans to refuse to wear a safety helmet on building sites, even where it is compulsory for all other workers. However, if they are injured in an accident they will only receive limited payment for damages. This will be based on an estimate of how badly they would have been hurt if they had been wearing a helmet.

- Is this a fair compromise?
- Or is it unfair that religious freedom should involve giving up other rights?

Should employers respect religion?

Religious faith can be the most valuable thing in some people's lives. It is therefore very important that they feel able to carry out the prayers and practices that their religion requires.

Not all employers have been sympathetic to these feelings. This has led to cases being brought before industrial tribunals and to changes in the law. In the UK and the USA, Muslim women have won the right to wear trousers instead of skirts with company uniforms, and Sikh men have won the right to wear beards – except where this breaks essential hygiene laws. Most faiths require that believers take part in public worship and attend services, rituals and special celebrations. Where these do not coincide with the holiday times of the majority community, some employers have been unwilling to allow workers time off.

In 1996, a tribunal ruled against a company which refused to let workers take a half-day off for the important Muslim festival of Eid. Employers who fail to make 'reasonable' arrangements with their Muslim employees for daily prayers or to allow Jewish people not to work on Saturdays, also run the risk of discrimination claims.

Does religion limit job choice?

Religion can limit job choice in a variety of ways. According to traditional Hindu beliefs, some jobs are 'unclean' and can only be performed by people from low castes (social and religious ranks in society). People who do these jobs are not allowed to take on any others, for fear the things they touch might also become ritually 'unclean'.

One group of Scottish fishermen, who belonged to a Christian sect, refused to eat with non-believers – even on board crowded fishing boats. Perhaps not surprisingly, they found it hard to get jobs. But from their point of view this was discrimination.

In the 1990s, the Taliban rulers of Afghanistan – on religious, not gender, grounds – banned women from working outside the home, even in institutions such as hospitals and girls' schools. As a result, thousands of women lost their jobs. Many sick women and girls also died, since the Taliban refused to allow male doctors to treat them.

Islam teaches that men and women should dress modestly. But extreme interpretations of the Muslim faith, like that practised by the Taliban rulers of Afghanistan, force women to cover themselves completely.

Are People With Disabilities Given Equal Opportunities?

In modern, industrialized countries, people with disabilities do not receive equal opportunities to gain paid employment. The situation is even worse in developing nations, where poverty and lack of modern technology make it harder for disabled people to find work.

IN TRADITIONAL SOCIETIES, physical or learning disabilities are often seen as a cause of shame. People with disabilities are shut away from view and do not come into contact with other members of the community. Some parents think there is no point in sending disabled children to school or helping them learn to share in household tasks or any other kind of work.

These attitudes existed until very recently all round the world. In the developed world, some equal opportunities campaigners are still campaigning to abolish separate schools for disabled children. They argue that these cut off disabled children from their peers and allow attitudes of ignorance and prejudice to persist throughout

This blind man was photographed in 1999 begging for food and money in Russia. Russia is one of many countries in which people with physical and mental impairment find it very difficult to get work and have to struggle to survive.

New technology helps people with hearing difficulties communicate in many different ways. But some employers are still reluctant to make full use of technology to allow disabled people to fulfil their potential.

the community. They also claim that separate schools deny children the chance to reach their full academic potential – though some teachers and parents do not agree.

Even when they have received an education, and can find a job, people with disabilities are most likely to be offered jobs in low-status, low-paid occupations. Significantly, it is hard to find up-to-date statistics from official sources. But in 1988 in the UK, full-time male disabled workers earned only 81 per cent of the pay of full-time male workers without disabilities doing equal work.

Why does this discrimination exist?

In the twenty-first century, there are computers and other electronic devices, such as sophisticated communications aids, which mean that more disabled people than in the past can make full use of their intellectual abilities and creative skills. Medical advances also mean that many people with disabilities are able to expect a longer and healthier life than ever before. Yet many employers are still reluctant to recruit disabled people and are sometimes quick to dismiss them when health problems arise.

Many disabled people would argue that they are not a 'problem' for employers to cope with, but that the real 'problem' lies in employers' negative attitudes towards them. Recently, some people with physical or mental conditions that affect their everyday lives have strongly objected to being described as 'disabled' or 'having disabilities'. They prefer to use the word 'impairment' to describe their condition. They argue that the real 'disabilities' they face are the limitations placed on them by society, employers and other individuals.

Why is the workplace unsuitable?

People with disabilities say that having a job is an important sign that they are being treated as full members of the community. Trying to find work can therefore be a key part of a larger fight for equality.

The sky is the limit

'We spend billions of dollars, yen, deutschmarks and pounds every year providing non-flyers with the most sophisticated mobility aids imaginable. They are called aeroplanes. An aeroplane is a mobility aid for non-flyers in exactly the same way as a wheelchair is a mobility aid for non-walkers...

We spend at least as much money to provide environments, usually called runways and airports, to ensure that these mobility aids can operate without hindrance... Non-walkers are treated in exactly the opposite way. Environments are often designed to exclude us, transport systems that claim to be public continue to deny us access and when we protest, we are told there is no money.'

Source: M. Oliver, Understanding Disability, From Theory to Practice

However, as well as facing negative attitudes, people with disabilities often have to struggle against an unsuitable environment. Until recently, many offices, shops and factories had steep steps and narrow doorways, unsuitable for wheelchair access.

One student complained, for example, that the entrance to her university's library was through a heavy revolving door. There was a smaller door which her wheelchair could get through, but library staff had to leave their other

Even modern buildings are often designed without consideration for people with disabilities. But with a little thought, it should be possible to allow disabled people equal access to all public buildings, shops, offices and other places of work.

In 1997, wheelchair users in San Francisco, USA, blocked roads used by buses. They were protesting against problems of access to many public transport vehicles faced by people with disabilities.

duties to help her use it. This placed extra pressure on them, made her feel embarrassed and caused delays for other library users.

Have laws changed?

In many countries, equal opportunities laws now require employers to make 'reasonable adjustments' to buildings and work practices, to offer disabled people equal access. These adjustments are often quite simple: rearranging work-stations, fitting extra lights, allowing flexible hours of work or providing special parking spaces close to offices or factories.

Slowly, companies are realizing that it can be good business to adapt their buildings and ways of working to employ disabled staff – and attract disabled customers. By doing so, they find they have a larger number of talented applicants to choose from and they also increase their trade.

Is transport a problem?

Transport problems also make it difficult for many people with disabilities to find or keep jobs. This is especially true if they live in big cities where private car use is slow and expensive and even people without impairments find crowded buses and trains hard to use.

Campaigners for disabled peoples' rights argue that with care and a fair share of public money, transport difficulties could be solved. Until this happens, many disabled people who want a career are forced to work in segregated workshops or from home.

Do Older People Have A Right To Work?

In wealthy countries, most people retire when they reach 60 or 65. They receive a pension from the state or their employer or live on money they saved while they were at work. But should they have the right to keep working if they want to?

MANY SOCIETIES TRADITIONALLY valued older peoples' experience. This situation still exists in many poor countries, where people often have no choice but to work for their entire lives merely to survive. But in Western industrial societies, the age of a worker has been identified as a particular area of discrimination.

Who were the Gray Panthers?

In the USA, a group of old-age activists called the Gray Panthers demanded the same rights as younger people to be appointed to jobs or offered promotion. They complained about advertisements which included sentences such as 'People over 50 need not apply' or 'Bright young person wanted'.

This elderly man in India has to keep on working in order to survive. Although people in wealthy Western countries can look forward to a retirement pension, most countries are too poor to provide for older citizens in this way.

Senior citizens in Texas, USA, attend classes to learn computing and information technology skills.

The Gray Panthers took their name and many of their ideas from civil rights campaigners, especially the Black Power movement. The Panthers believed in absolute equality for all people, regardless of age, colour, disability or sex and thought that doing useful work gave meaning and purpose to everyone's life. Being denied the chance to work took these away.

Why do older workers suffer?

Discrimination against older workers becomes more serious during economic crises. Companies try to save money by reducing wage bills. Since older people are likely to be more senior, and therefore earning higher wages than younger staff, companies often try to make them redundant first.

There are also general prejudices against older workers. Some employers fear that they might be less familiar with modern technology. They might be physically less capable; and less willing to move house, adapt to fast-changing work practices or learn new skills.

But there are signs that attitudes are changing. Companies who have deliberately recruited older workers have found that they are particularly reliable and trustworthy. They have emotional maturity and a wider experience of life, which makes them better at coping with problems.

Older women, who have finished raising their families, are also less likely than younger women workers to need maternity leave. Employers who run shops also say that many customers appreciate the 'old-fashioned' courtesy of older staff.

Can We Achieve Equal Opportunities For All?

We are all potentially guilty of discrimination against people who seem different from ourselves or have fewer advantages than we do. Equal opportunities campaigners urge us to think carefully about all we do and say. They tell us to make sure we treat everyone we meet with equal fairness, consideration and courtesy.

CAMPAIGNERS USE THE slogan: 'If you are not part of the solution, you must be part of the problem.' Their argument is that individuals, businesses, institutions and of course governments should all act to ensure that everyone they deal with is treated fairly and equally.

Although the USA's Civil Rights Act, promising equal opportunities, became law in 1964, many citizens still experience discrimination. These women were photographed in 1982, protesting for equality.

DEBATE - Do you agree with the following statement?

'The tide of discrimination... is so strong that, unless we actively swim against it, it is more or less inevitable that we will be carried along with it.'

Source: Neil Thompson, Anti-discriminatory Practice, British Association for Social Work

Singer Bono and boxing champion Muhammad Ali support the launch of the Jubilee 2000 campaign for poor countries' debt relief.

Are equal opportunities a global problem?

Other campaigners urge us to look beyond the people we meet face to face and consider how our attitudes and actions affect people in countries around the world. The economies of rich and poor countries are now linked by globalization. So, the personal choices we make – for example, in what we choose to buy in the shops – can affect equal opportunities at work for the men, women and children in developing countries who make these products.

It is a sad fact that, while awareness of equal opportunities has increased in wealthy countries, the gap between rich and poor nations has widened. Author Joni Seager stated: 'Since the 1960s, the poorest 20 per cent of the world's population have seen their share of global income decline from 2.3 per cent to 1.4 per cent, while the share of the richest 20 per cent rose from 70 per cent to 80 per cent.' Statistically, the poorest people in the world today are old women belonging to racial minority groups. They have suffered from a lifetime of discrimination and unequal opportunities.

Yet there are signs of hope. International campaigning groups such as Jubilee 2000 have demanded the cancellation of debts owed by poor countries to rich ones. They hope this will leave poor countries free to improve education and healthcare – and to introduce equal opportunities policies, if they choose.

In wealthy developed countries, tribunal cases like Neil Walkingshaw's, described at the beginning of this book, have shown how equal opportunities laws can help to make life better for many ordinary families, whatever work they do.

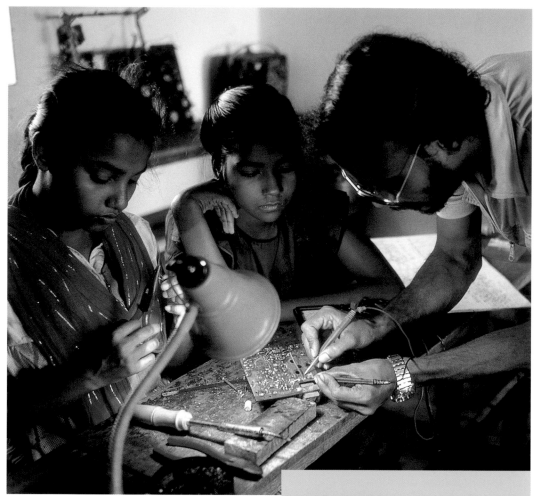

Education helps offer women in the developing world equal opportunities to learn skills. These women in Bangalore, India, are attending an electronics class.

Is education the answer?

Most people would agree that education is one of the most important and effective ways of changing peoples' lives. It allows students to learn skills, gain knowledge and win qualifications.

However, as we have seen in this book, getting a good education does not guarantee equal opportunities at work. Well-qualified candidates from disadvantaged groups still find it harder to get the jobs they want than applicants

Learning together

'I have a disability caused by polio... I try to convince disabled children to go to school.
I organize meetings with parents and with children. If we unite all disabled children then we can raise our voices and get what we need – an education.'

Source: Khim Bahadur, aged 17, Nepal, from the Save the Children Annual Review 2000–2001

from majority groups. But there are signs that employers are beginning to recognize that well educated people – whatever their background – are too valuable to turn away.

In the UK, the proportion of men holding top jobs (officially defined as professional, managerial and employers) is now the same for men of Chinese, African, Asian and Indian ethnic origin as it is for whites. What is more, men with A-levels from all minority ethnic groups, except Afro-Caribbeans, are more likely than white men to be in professional jobs.

In 2001, students at Bombay University, India, took part in a torchlight rally to campaign for equal educational rights for all Indian children. They wanted other young people to have the same opportunities as themselves.

Are women receiving equal opportunities?

Well-qualified women still face discrimination, even in educational careers. In the UK in 1995, for example, women held 49 per cent of all teaching posts in secondary schools, but only 30 per cent of senior positions such as head or deputy-head teachers.

In developing countries, a good education can be even more important in escaping poverty and winning the chance of a good career. And in developing countries, the shortage of skilled professional people can sometimes lead to more equal opportunities for women than in rich industrialized nations. For example, there is a higher percentage of female university teachers in Namibia, Bulgaria and St Lucia in the Caribbean, than there is in Australia, Spain or the UK.

How do people protest?

Some campaigners stage protests to try to educate people about how their purchasing decisions affect local workers' lives. Some of these protests can be deeply controversial, such as the riots at international economic summits, held from 1999 to 2001 in the USA, Sweden and Italy. Demonstrators protested against wealthy governments' economic policies, the influence of the World Trade Organization and the power of multinational corporations. Their aim was to show solidarity with poor and disadvantaged peoples worldwide. But the protests were marred by violence.

There are no easy answers to the problems of poverty and injustice. But by asking questions and putting forward their own points of view, peaceful campaigners and educators hope to make people aware of the importance of equal opportunities around the world.

REFERENCE

LAWS, CODES AND TREATIES

UNITED KINGDOM

DISABILITY DISCRIMINATION

*The Disabled Persons (Employment)
Acts 1944 and 1958*
Set up a quota system of 3 per cent
disabled employees for large companies.

*Chronically Sick and Disabled Persons
Act 1970*
Gave disabled people equal rights of
access to public buildings, special needs
housing and social services.

Education Act 1981
Encouraged integrated education for
pupils with physical impairment or
learning difficulties.

Building Act 1984
Introduced new standards for buildings
to give disabled people better access.

Companies Act 1985
Large companies instructed to report on
policies for employing disabled staff.

*Disabled Persons (Services, Consultation
and Representation) Act 1986*
Gave disabled people some rights to be
consulted on services provided.

Disability Discrimination Act 1995
Made it unlawful for large companies to
discriminate against disabled job
applicants; ordered improved rights of
access to buildings, services and public
transport; set up National Disability
Council; gave disabled people the right
to bring cases of discrimination before
industrial tribunals.

Disability Rights Commission Act 1999
Set up Disability Rights Commission,
which had stronger powers than the
previous National Disability Council.
It also had the duty to work towards the
elimination of discrimination, promote
equal opportunities, encourage good
practice and monitor the working of the
Disability Discrimination Act of 1995.

SEX DISCRIMINATION

Equal Pay Act 1970
Stated that women could claim equal
pay with men for equal work and
complain to industrial tribunals if they
faced discrimination.

Sex Discrimination Act 1975
Banned discrimination on grounds of
sex or marital status at work, in training
and education, in providing goods and
services. Gave employees the right to
take cases to industrial tribunals.

*Employment Protection (Part-Time
Employees) Regulations 1995*
Gave part-time workers many of the
same legal rights as full-time workers.

Employment Rights Act 1996
Gave women rights to claim maternity
leave, maternity pay and (under certain
conditions) to return to work after the
birth of a child.

RACIAL DISCRIMINATION

Race Relations Act 1965
Banned racial discrimination in public places.

Race Relations Act 1968
Banned racial discrimination in housing and employment.

Race Relations Act 1976
Banned discrimination on grounds of colour, race, nationality, ethnic or national origins – at work, in training and education, in providing goods and services. Set up Commission for Racial Equality to enforce laws.

Local Government Act 1988
Placed a general duty on local authorities to end unlawful racial discrimination.

Race Relations (Remedies) Act 1994
Gave industrial tribunals the power to award unlimited compensation to victims of race discrimination.

RELIGIOUS DISCRIMINATION

Fair Employment Protection Act (Northern Ireland) 1976
Banned discrimination on grounds of religion in large companies; introduced monitoring of religious composition of staff and compulsory anti-discrimination recruitment policies. Enforced by Fair Employment Commission.

CODES OF PRACTICE

These provide guidance to employers and others on how to put anti-discrimination laws into practice. The three codes are very powerful – their recommendations have to be taken into account by industrial tribunals:

Equal Opportunities Commission Statutory Code of Practice, introduced 1985.

Commission for Racial Equality Statutory Code of Practice, introduced 1984.

Disability Rights Commission Statutory Code of Practice, introduced 2000.

EUROPE

EUROPEAN TREATIES AND CONVENTIONS RELATING TO EQUAL RIGHTS

European Human Rights Convention 1950
Added the main points of the United
Nations Declaration of Human Rights to
European law, including:
- the right to life and liberty
- the right to a fair trial
- the right to respect for home and
  family life
- the right to personal privacy
- freedom of conscience [beliefs and
  ideas]
- freedom of association [attending
  meetings, forming groups].

Treaty of Rome 1957
Required governments of member states
to ensure that men and women receive
equal pay for equal work.

EUROPEAN COMMISSION DIRECTIVES RELATING TO EQUAL OPPORTUNITIES AT WORK

Equal Pay Directive 1975
Clarified rules on equal pay for men
and women laid down in Treaty of
Rome 1957.

Equal Treatment Directive 1976
Stated that men and women should
receive equal treatment in work
conditions, access to training,
promotion and dismissal.

*Recommendations on the Protection of the
Dignity of Women and Men at Work and
Code of Practice on Measures to Combat
Sexual Harassment 1991   .*
Banned sexual harassment of any kind
at work.

Pregnant Workers Directive 1992
Stated that a pregnant woman should
not be dismissed from her job except in
exceptional circumstances unconnected
with her pregnancy.

Parental Leave Directive 1996
Gave men and women the right to
unpaid parental leave for up to three
months after the birth or adoption of
a child.
(This does not automatically apply in
the UK.)

FROM THE EUROPEAN SOCIAL CHARTER ON FUNDAMENTAL SOCIAL RIGHTS 1992 (PART OF THE MAASTRICHT TREATY)

Article 19
'Equal treatment for men and women shall be assured. Equal opportunities for men and women shall be developed.'

Article 29
'All disabled persons, whatever the origin and nature of their disablement, shall be entitled to additional concrete measures aimed at improving their social and professional integration. These measures shall concern… vocational training, ergonomics, accessibility, mobility, means of transport and housing.'

USA

MOST IMPORTANT LAWS RELATING TO EQUAL OPPORTUNITIES AT WORK

Equal Pay Act 1963
Stated that men and women doing equal jobs should receive equal pay.

Civil Rights Act 1964
Banned discrimination on grounds of race, colour, religion, sex or national origin.

Age Discrimination in Employment Act 1967
Protected people 40 years and older from job discrimination.

Rehabilitation Act 1973
Banned discrimination in government jobs against qualified people with disabilities.

Americans with Disabilities Act 1990
Banned discrimination in all jobs against qualified people with disabilities.

Civil Rights Act 1991
Provided for financial damages where people could prove job discrimination.

GLOSSARY

amendment Change or addition to law or other important document.

apartheid 'Apart-ness', the South African government policy of strict racial separation, in force from 1948 to 1991.

atheist Someone who does not believe in any god or gods.

board member One of the top managers in a company.

British Empire Lands conquered and ruled by Britain.

capitalist Capitalists believe that private companies and individuals should control the creation, distribution (sharing out) and exchange of wealth, without interference from the state.

civil rights Legal rights that safeguard political freedom and individual liberty.

Civil Service The men and women who work for the government. Their jobs include giving advice to ministers, planning new laws, collecting taxes.

communist Communists believe that all property and power should belong to the nation and that each citizen should work for the common good, not for their family or themselves.

Constitution A collection of laws, made in 1787, which defined the powers of the government of the USA and how they should be used.

co-operative schemes Social or economic activities designed to help local communities or groups of workers. They are planned and managed by members, who share any profits.

damages Money paid to people whose lives have been damaged by acts that are against the law, such as discrimination.

discrimination Treating some groups of people less well than others.

dissidents People who protest against government policies.

ergonomics The scientific study of how people interact with their surroundings.

ethnic minorities Groups of people with different racial or national origins from the majority of citizens in the country where they live.

family wage A wage traditionally designed to support a working man, his wife and their children.

feminists People who campaign for women to be equally respected and valued with men.

free market An economy where prices and wages are not controlled by the government.

gender Whether a person is male or female.

gender roles The typical behaviour expected of men and women by their community and their religious faith.

globalization Close trading links between countries around the world that developed rapidly in the late twentieth century.

immigrants People who have come into a new country after leaving their original homeland.

inheritance laws Laws which govern how property may be passed from parents to their children.

institutional racism Policies and procedures in institutions that deny equal treatment to members of ethnic minority groups.

international economic summits Meetings of government and business leaders held to discuss worldwide economic problems.

left-wing Holding strong socialist views. Socialists believe that the state should limit extremes of individual wealth and poverty and encourage equality of income, employment and opportunity among all citizens.

liberal Supporting justice, tolerance and personal freedom.

marital status Whether a person is married, single or divorced.

multinational corporations Large businesses that operate in many different countries.

norm Accepted standard of behaviour.

peers Equals, people of the same age.

pension Money paid to people who are too old or ill to work any more. Money to pay pensions comes from companies, government insurance schemes and workers' own savings.

piecework Work where payment is based on the number of goods produced, rather than on the time taken.

progressive Willing to use new ideas.

public administration The running of government and other state institutions, such as health and education services.

retailing Buying and selling.

siblings Brothers and sisters.

Soviet Union A vast, very powerful nation, containing 15 separate states in Eastern Europe and Northern Asia, which was founded after the Russian Revolution of 1917. It was run by communist governments until its collapse in 1991.

stereotyping Grouping people of similar age, ethnic origin or nationality together, as if they were all the same, and judging them on the basis of limited information or opinions.

taboos Traditional religious rules that prohibit certain actions.

trade unions Associations of working men and women, who join together to protect their rights, campaign for better pay and conditions and provide education and welfare benefits for members.

welfare state A state in which the government provides health, education and welfare services for all citizens 'from the cradle to the grave'. Usually, these are paid for by taxes.

women's movement Campaigning movement by feminists and other women to win equal rights and equal opportunities with men.

FURTHER INFORMATION

BOOKS

Freedom! by Amnesty International
(Human Rights Education Pack,
Hodder, 2001)

Stand Up for Your Rights! by Peace Child
International (Two-Can Publishing, 2000)

This is Citizenship!, Book 1 by T and J
Fiehn (John Murray, 2002)

What's at Issue? Citizenship and You by
Katrina Dunbar (Heinemann, 2000)

What's at Issue? Human Rights by Paul
Wignell (Heinemann, 2001)

What's at Issue? Prejudice and Difference
by Paul Wignell (Heinemann, 2000)

Young Citizen's Passport by the
Citizenship Foundation (Hodder, 2002)

SOURCES

Anti-Discriminatory Practice by Neil
Thompson (British Association of Social
Workers/Palgrave, 2001)

*Discrimination in the Workplace, A
Practical Guide* by Julian Hemming (ed)
(John Wiley and Sons, 1997)

Equal Opportunities and Social Policy
by Barbara Bagilhole (Longman, 1997)

The State of Women in the World Atlas
by Joni Seager (Penguin, 1997)

*Understanding Disability, From Theory to
Practice* by M Oliver (Macmillan, 1996)

Women, Work and Equal Opportunities by
Barbara Bagilhome (Avebury, 1994)

UK ORGANIZATIONS

GOVERNMENT ORGANIZATIONS

**The Commission for Racial Equality
(CRE England)**
Elliott House, 10/12 Allington Street
London SW1E 5EH
www.cre.gov.uk

CRE Scotland
Hanover House, 45–51 Hanover Street
Edinburgh EH2 2PJ
www.cre.gov.uk

CRE Wales
14th Floor, Capital Tower,
Greyfriars Road, Cardiff CF1 3AG
www.cre.gov.uk

**The Equal Opportunities Commission
(EOC England)**
Arndale House, Arndale Centre
Manchester M4 3EQ
www.eoc.org.uk

EOC Scotland
St Stephens House, 279 Bath Street
Glasgow G2 4JL
www.eoc.org.uk

EOC Wales
Windsor House, Windsor Lane
Cardiff CF10 3GE
www.eoc.org.uk

Disability Rights Commission
DRC Helpline, Freepost MID 02164
Stratford-upon-Avon CV37 9BR
www.drc-gb.org

Women's National Commission
Cabinet Office, 1st Floor, 35 Great Smith
Street, London SW1P 3BQ
www.thewnc.org.uk

INTERNATIONAL ORGANIZATIONS

United Nations Organization UK
3 Whitehall Court, London SW1A 2EL
www.una-uk.org

United Nations Children's Fund (UNICEF)
Africa House, 64-78 Kingsway
London WC2B 6NB
www.unicef.org

Jubllee Plus
The New Economics Foundation
Cinnamon House, 6-8 Cole Street
London SE1 4YH

VOLUNTARY ORGANIZATIONS

For information on voluntary organizations that work or campaign for equal opportunities, contact:

National Council for Voluntary Organizations (NCVO)
Regent's Wharf, 8 All Saints Street
London NR1 9RL
www.ncvo-vol.org.uk

Scottish Council for Voluntary Organizations
18/19 Claremont Crescent
Edinburgh EH7 4QD
www.scvo.org.uk

USA ORGANIZATIONS

Equal Employment Opportunity Commission
Publications Distribution Center
PO Box 12549 Cincinnati,
Ohio 45212-0549
www.eeoc.gov

WEBSITES

www.tiger.gov.uk
A UK government site that describes itself as 'a user-friendly guide to employment law'. 'Tiger' is short for 'Tailored Interactive Guidance on Employment Rights'.

www.mobility-unit.detr.gov.uk
A UK government site – home page of the Mobility and Inclusion Unit at the Department of the Environment, Transport and the Regions.

www.labournet.org
International site listing workers' campaigning groups worldwide.

www.now.org
Site run by the National Organization of Women USA, with links to women's organizations in many countries.

www.womenlobby.org
Home site of the European Women's Lobby, with links to many other women's sites worldwide.

www.dial.org.uk
Site with a very great deal of information about groups working for disabled people and disability rights.

www.seniorsnetwork.co.uk
Information about groups campaigning for older peoples' rights in the UK.

www.graypanthers.org
Site run by organization campaigning for older peoples' rights in the USA.

www.eeoc.gov/facts/qanda
Laws prohibiting job discrimination in the USA, by the Equal Employment Opportunities Commission.

INDEX